I Was a Lesbian

I Was a Lesbian

Holli J. Hunt

To order additional copies of this book, contact:
Xlibris Corporation
1-888-795-4274
www.Xlibris.com
Orders@Xlibris.com
60060

CONTENTS

CHAPTER 1

"The Underdog"

It's like 1 o'clock in the morning on a cool summer day; my home girl and I are hangin out in the front of our apartment building sipping some coolers and smoking weed. My home girl has this crazy look on her face and she says "Girl ain't that your man zooming by in his car and it looked like to me he had some light skinned chic in there with him. I turn around and see the car zooming by but I said "no you probably just trippin". That situation just didn't sit well with me so I called him on his cell phone. He answered and said he was at his mom's house in the bed. While I'm on the phone with him I jump in my car and jump on the e-way headed to his mom's house. We pull up and just as my home girl had thought, it was true, he had some chic in the car with him. I was furious but I didn't even say anything to him, I turned around and went back home. The next day in the evening time, he called me and I wouldn't answer. Soon afterwards he was pulling up in front of my house. I was already out front when he pulled up and I just ignored him. He kept saying come here and I wouldn't. That was it for me! I just couldn't take no more. It was time I got rid of this zero and that I did!

I thought about how to write what I needed to say over and over again. Until I realized that somebody needed to hear my story and come to understand what they have and are experiencing, can be conquered. There was no other way to say this but to come from my heart with the unadulterated truth.

Choosing to be a lesbian is a choice we make, this is not who we are. In spite of what TV, society or Hollywood says, we are not born gay. I didn't understand the behavior I displayed, to me it became the thing to do, the way to be and there was this inner cry that I couldn't allow anyone to hear or see. This lifestyle came upon me while I was in a vulnerable and disgusted phase in my life. I began to make choices like I didn't care anymore about nothing and nobody. I had just walked away from a crazy relationship where the man I was sleeping with was cheating and playing a lot of mind games and I was fed up.

It was never a healthy relationship, we just got together late at night and was intimate. My major concern and law had been not to sleep with anyone that was sleeping around, so that had to be agreed upon before I ever agreed to be in the relationship. He was the type that didn't care about family, he just wanted what he wanted and that was sex. When I met him I had 2 children, he never expressed a desire to spend time with me and my boys, it was just always coming around at night to score and then be on his way without a care in the world. Well, I played a part in this relationship and that was just having sex. I spent most of my time with my boys and selling drugs all day and night so it was like all I really wanted out of this relationship. But I didn't tolerate sleeping with a man who slept around. That was not my style. It never took more than one at a time for me. So if a man cheated, that was like going against the grain! A big NO-NO and I wasn't having it. Nevertheless, the only beautiful thing that our relationship produced was our son Donnell; a precious gift from God. To make matters worse, prior to this relationship, I had been in a violently abusive relationship for years. This relationship was my first love. In the beginning things were beautiful. I thought he was a sweetheart by the way he would treat me and there was this nerdy type about him I was attracted to. As time progressed; he began to verbally and physically abuse me as if I were a stranger on the street. I was basically treated like a prisoner; he began to demand that I stay in the house and raise our children. "You belong in the house with these kids" he would say. So life for me was very limited to the inside and I never had much contact with my family and friends. When I did have the company of family and friends, he would be so rude and disrespectful til they would leave. Even if we were together outside of the house and I would run into an old friend, I would speak and maybe hug them. Later on, that was a beat down. When we met we were both very young and soon after that I got pregnant. We didn't get together right away; I made him work hard to get me. Anyway, I was sort of spending time with another guy, sneaking and having sex at the age of 15 not knowing a thing about sex and the consequences.

As a result, I got pregnant. He was the honorable type; he still wanted to raise my son as his own. Eventually, we got together and I was convinced he was a good guy. As time progressed, we had a son together and he arrived 14 months after my first born son. Things began to change. He began to verbally and physically abuse me on a consistent basis. Things got ugly and I suffered a lot of abuse and my children were also there to witness every blow and stomp, Steven Segal style whippings. You see he was a big fan of Steven Segal, we used to watch his movies while smoking weed and drinking. Later on, when he got mad at me, he would use all of Steven Segal's moves on me. One day I built up enough courage to put an end to this life as I knew it, without a care in the world.

I started defending myself verbally, then I would pick up things like knives, lamps, and bottles whatever was close to me I would use it to get him off me. If I felt he was gonna hit me, I would go for him first to beat him to the punch. Yeah I tried to leave many times but he would not allow that, he'd just show up and convince me that I needed to come back to him, using threats to provoke me to come back, and I each time I would. I loved him dearly and I would even make excuses for him when friends and family would say things about him and our relationship.

I didn't understand the kind of love that I had for him that caused me to love him in spite of how he treated me. When the abuse began I was afraid, and wouldn't dare attempt to defend myself. That's kinda hard to believe if you knew me personally. I was the neighborhood rough neck how could I be afraid of anybody? The more and more abuse I took, I started getting angrier. Then I began to say to myself "enough is enough". What really got me to thinking it was truly time for me to leave was when a very close friend of mine cried to me one day while we were sitting around smoking weed and drinking. At first I said you're just trippin off that weed. But I could see how serious she was. She was really crying and said that she was really scared for me. After this, I began to plan my escape. It was as if a lightbulb switch had just come on in my mind and I was truly ready to get away. The only way I got away from this relationship was with me defending myself violently. I never wanted things to end this way. I stabbed him with the biggest knife I could find in my mothers' kitchen. The knife was to scare him off, but he was not the type to easily scare. Before I knew it, I had really hurt him, the man I loved and cared so much about. Deep down inside I was hurting too after that incident and I knew that I couldn't go back. I knew in my heart that things between us would never be the same. I even went to visit him in the hospital, I didn't know that things were this bad. I was so sad when I saw how he could've lost his life. He couldn't even speak. After experiencing so much hurt and disappointment from men I was mad, angry, and disappointed. At the same time I felt free, free to do what I pleased and that I did. Early on after these relationships, I didn't realize my emotions were unstable and that the choices I made after these circumstances would cause more hurt and lead to more hurtful and unhealthy relationships. I didn't know that I would need to heal from my wounds and then move on with my life. I just moved on and made choices from my scarred emotions.

MY CHILDHOOD

I grew up in the Ida B. Wells project, on the south side of Chicago, where crime was like a normal part of life. Although the neighborhood was filled with poor and struggling African Americans, my childhood was wonderful. I remember being very active as a child, I had an enormous love for dancing, singing and sports. That love still burns deep inside of me. I spent most of my time indulging in those activities on a daily basis.

If I wasn't at the neighborhood community center swimming, playing ping pong, taking dancing lessons, playing basketball, or shooting pool, I was in our backyard playing strike-out, softball, baseball, football or playing the old school games like red light green light, shooting marbles or hang go seek. One of my most favorite things to do was to play video games. Mrs. Pacman and Millipede were my favorite. My siblings and I would go to this candy store and play games all day long. My mom would give us all lots of quarters to have a good time. This was one of the hangout spots for all the kids in the neighborhood. It was like heaven. I was most fond of playing strike-out. This was a game where we would paint a box on the wall and a big x on the inside of the box and we would stand against the box with a bat while the pitcher would stand about 25 feet away and pitch the ball as fast as he could. I was very good at it. I enjoyed hitting the ball as far as my eyes could follow. I was always the only girl playing strike-out. Basketball was my first love though, I loved to shoot hoops. I was very good at it and very quick. I could shoot the ball from three point range very good. Most days I would be on the basketball court for hours. Those were the good old days to me. When I reminisce about those days all I can ever do is smile. Meanwhile, the environment and the immediate people that I was surrounded by played a major part in the choices I began to make and those choices contributed greatly to the woman I am today.

I had the greatest mother, Charolette Jackson, she was a beautiful woman with the heart of a tiger and a crazy sense of humor. She raised 12 children with great discipline and she was great at it. She would give this look and we knew she meant business. A single parent left to handle it all on her own and yet she managed. She was a real superwoman. We had the best of everything. She could cook like nobody's business. She had so many hidden gifts and talents that I recognize now then I ever could have seen before.

She had the kind of personality where people loved to be around her and eat her good cooking. She was that strong tower that exemplified strength for her family. She would have card games and have lots of friends over eating, listening to music and playing cards. She would always call me and my brothers downstairs and have us to dance for her company. I was a very good dancer. I used to imitate Michael Jackson very good and my mom loved to see her kids dance. We would meet all kinds of people when my mom had these card games. They were held quite often. My mom was such a special lady. She taught us with her actions how to prioritize our lives and do what it takes to get the job done. Back when I was younger I never understood why she made some of the choices she made. Like being very strict about cleanliness, demanding us to be presentable in appearance, didn't accept bad grades from us in school, and doing the best with what she had.

She taught us long ago about making lemonade when life throws a lemon our way. She never was the verbally expressive kind unless she got angry; her actions spoke volumes to all who watched her. But somewhere down the road, tough circumstances showed up and she allowed those circumstances to overshadow that bright light she housed.

I remember getting evicted from our apartment in the projects. It seemed that things began to go down hill ever since that day. Our family began to face some horrible situations. We had to move into an apartment that my father owned and he treated us like we were his prisoners. He really dogged us out. I guess this was a way to hurt my mother for whatever reason. Instead of reaching out to his family, he took the opportunity to trample over us as if we were nothing. Some how these trying times began to get the best of my mother and the glue that held our family together was slowly unraveling. We began to move around a lot, moving in with friends and family members. And as a result, the family began to make divisive choices. It was as if there was no sense of direction and there was no one to guide us.

My mom was there but she just began to stop living and hope was absent. It was as if she had succumb to the circumstances of life and they trampled over her and got victory.

My mom passed away in 1994 while I was just 20 years old. The family was left with no direction and a lifetime of pain.

I believe stress and worrying was truly the cause of her death. She was also afraid to visit the doctor. She began to allow the spirit of fear to take resident inside her and it annihilated all that she once stood for and believed. Although she was diagnosed with Tuberculosis, I believe in my heart that it was not the root of the problem. Now that she's gone, I've declared to allow her to live on through me. That tenacious spirit that she once possessed, that spirit of a tiger, I have released that spirit from within me in her honor. With this spirit mountains will be moved and generations will be changed. I will live with her in mind every step of the way and continue to pass down this spirit of life and love.

Now my father, Charles Goods was a very gifted and talented man. The only child and got everything his little heart desired from his parents. He was a very well educated and very handsome guy. He was chief of the police department. He was very gifted with his hands; he could do all kinds of maintenance work and he was basically the all around Mr. fix-it kind of guy. I never really knew my father on a personal level. I only remember seeing him periodically. The last time I remember him being around on a consistent basis, I was about three years old. I remember sitting on his lap having a conversation with him. You see I was the daddy's little girl type. My mom used to say all the time that I looked just like him all I needed was a mustache. I was crazy about my dad. As I got older I started to see and understand that my dad was not present in our lives like we needed him to be and that crazy love I once had for him turned into hate.

I wanted him to be a part of my life but he made other choices. This unhealthy relationship between myself and my dad caused me a lot of hurt. I remember hurling out hateful things to him when he would show up, I would even spit at his feet. In my heart the hurt was real, but I would pretend that I didn't care because I didn't know how to deal with the pain I was feeling.

My dad was not only talented and handsome; he was verbally and physically abusive to my mother. He housed the spirit of lust that dominated his choices and ultimately his behavior. He had kids all over town.

I still haven't met some of my sisters and brothers on his side of the family. He would do his dirt and come home and take out his frustrations on my mother like blacking her eye or chasing her with an ax. He got very physical with her quite often.

As time progressed, I got older and wiser, I learned how crucial it was for me to forgive my dad and love him in spite of the relationship we never had and in spite the love I didn't receive from him. I still wanted to be a part of his life and I hoped that he felt the same as I did.

We were cordial for quite some time and for the last year of his life, we started to smile with one another and enjoy each other's presence.

My dad got sick and he needed someone to care for him and I really wanted to be there for him but there wasn't much I could do for him at this point but pray. When my dad passed away in 2006, forgiveness allowed me to be at peace with the situation because I had apologized to him for all the hateful and cruel things I said and did to him. I'm glad that I had learned how crucial it is to love the ones God put in your life no matter their mistakes, mishaps or shortcomings.

I was able to thank God for the man He allowed to be my earthly father. Now, he too lives on through me with the spirit of "peace and love". I quote peace and love because those were the words he would use when he answered his telephone. I still quote some of his pet names he had for us like darling dear, dirt dobbler, bad but and wee-hart. That's one of the ways I share the love I had for him with my siblings. I have a beautiful family. My sisters and brothers are all very talented and gifted. We all have a special love for one another. We are all striving to make choices as a unit to make this family better and stronger. A family that demonstrates love and peace to one another and all we encounter. Yes we have our ups and downs like any other family, somehow we put aside our differences and show up when one of us needs some help. That's what family is about: Being there for one another.

In the meantime, during the course of time before my mom was sick but my dad was still missing in action, I began to make choices concerning the desire to have a better and greater life for myself and family. I'm now 14 years old and living with my sister and her older boyfriend. This was the year everything changed in my life. My older brother had passed away, Charles Mckee "Poody" we would call him. He was such an inspiration for our family, very smart, could play baseball and basketball very good, handsome and unique in the choices he made. He was the lady's man. The fatherly type that loved his son and family very much. He passed away due to a drug overdose. This was quite shocking because he was known for the one to sell all the drugs not just locally but in other states as well. For him to die using drugs was and still is a mystery to me. I had never seen my mom so sad and discombobulated. This really delivered a strong blow to her heart. She was hurt immensely. This was like adding fuel to the flame when it came to that light of hers going dim. Shortly after that I got pregnant. The tomboy of the times and here I am only 15 years old and pregnant.

I was so afraid, I couldn't even face my mother, and my sister had to be the one to tell her. I thank God today for the way she handled the news. She never turned her back on me or said anything hurtful, she just loved me anyhow. That was true love. Well, I informed my baby's daddy about the news and he wanted no part of it so he ran like a cheetah. We first met when we were a few years younger, we was on the same baseball team together, The Pittsburg Pirates. I was the only girl on the team. I remember getting up to the bat and the pitcher would lob me the ball because he knew I was a girl and he would be teasing me. So I would tell the coach and then the coach would tell his coach to pitch to me like he pitched to everybody else. So as soon as he would throw the first pitch, I would knock the ball out of sight. And all his teammates would laugh and say "Man, you let a girl hit your stuff." I had a lot of fun on that team being the only girl. I would wear my hat all the way down on my head so that other teams couldn't recognize I was a girl, then I would hit a home run and take my hat off. They would say hecky nall, that's a girl! We attended the same grammar school together. He would walk me home from school and was very sweet yet he had this humorous side that I loved. We started sneaking and having sex. He would climb out his momma's window to come over and see me. I remember on many occasions how his momma would come to our house and take him home by the ear. But when I found out I was pregnant, he changed like the weather! Now I'm left to have a baby without his father.

Nevertheless, I had begun a relationship with my first love and he wanted to raise my unborn son as his son. I thought that was wonderful.

This was one of the reasons why I loved and respected his so much. I brought my first born into the world, a bouncing baby boy; Kerron Rasheem Hunt. He was a cutie.

All the nurses in the hospital took his picture and kept saying he was cute enough to be a girl. I was young and confused, I knew nothing about raising a baby, and I was still a baby myself. Thank God for a mom with experience. She helped me so much and she was really the one who raised my boys. Meanwhile, this behavior of abuse became the behavior I accepted. Instead of being in a relationship where the man would love and care for me I now behaved like my mother and accepted an abusive man. I never knew that I would take on the behavior of my mother and father and that low self-esteem and lust was seeking to destroy me from the inside out.

It seems that a pattern had been established in our family. We all struggled with low self-esteem and we all began to succumb to lust and these spirits would ultimately guide our choices. This pattern throughout the family was designed by the enemy to cause nothing but hurt, pain, and destruction. These spirits sought to pervert the God given spirits we were born with. What I mean by pervert is cause me, my siblings and anyone to do the complete opposite of what we were created to do. Persuade us to take our God given spirits and use them to do harm to ourselves and others when we were suppose to use them so that others could benefit in positive ways. The spirits that would cause us to have life and have it more abundantly like love, peace, joy, and righteousness. My siblings and I are all gifted in the areas of sports, art, music, cosmetology, entrepreneurship, and so much more. I understand that I was born with a God given aggressive spirit. The enemy has been trying to pervert it in every way possible since I was born so that I and others wouldn't benefit from it. This aggressive spirit is the kind of spirit that keeps an attitude of a tiger, an optimist, tenacious, that "I believe I can fly" kind of spirit.

As a child I didn't know the spirit I housed, I didn't understand it. As I look back on my childhood days I can definitely see it in action. I could out do all the boys in sports and break dancing. I could do all the moves the break dancers were doing; I was the only girl on this dance team. We would have talent shows and when it was time for me to do a solo, the people would go crazy. I could pop-lock, do the helicopter, the crab-leg, foot-work, I could do it all! They were amazed at my ability to do all the same moves as the guys did. To me it was natural. I even beat up on a lot of boys, some much bigger than me. As I got older, that aggressive spirit along with low self-esteem began to dominate and persuade my choices. I began to gangbang at the age of 16, 17. I dropped out of school, started smoking marijuana and drinking and was nominated the first lady of the gang "gangster disciples" in my neighborhood.

During that time, I started selling drugs as a means to take care of my kids and family. To me this was the only way to get money to get the things we needed. It was what I was accustomed to, the only way I knew. I had watched my big brother do it and then my big sister the one I was staying with when I was 14 up until I was about 17. It was all around me, very heavy in the environment. I quickly learned the game. I even remember back when I was a little girl about 4 or 5, my older brother that's decease would take me and my nephew on "runs" with him.

He would use us to hold the drugs and money to be a distraction to those who were watching him. I got good at it (so I thought) and before I knew it I was in too deep to quit. The money was good and it was taking care of my children and me and the needs of my family. Things began to get out of control on my behalf. I started carrying a pistol everywhere I went and now it was my nephew and I like a team. We would watch each other's back. He had the master plan. It was as if he had made new rules to the game and these rules made bigger things happen for us. Not only in good ways but the police started to harass us and give us problems like making us take all our money out of our pockets and throwing it up in the air so anyone could take it. More problems would come our way as well.

Not only was I still gang bangin but I was a mother with kids and I remember leaving my kids at home with my mom on many occasions because I was doing my own thing and being the mother they needed me to be I didn't understand how to be at that time. I wanted to run the streets and do my thing. I would get cursed out a lot but all was on my mind was money and the lifestyle.

I was also in a relationship with an older guy that supplied me with all the drugs I wanted. He was like my 'sugar daddy'. It wasn't really a relationship, he just gave me everything I wanted and we would have sex periodically. Before long, I started going to jail for drug possessions, leaving my children behind for my mother to take care of them.

She barely made a way for herself, and yet she managed to be there for my boys. She was truly a tough woman. It hurts as I look back on my behavior and see how immature I was and the stupid choices I made.

I thought I had everything under control when actually I had no control. I was young and very naïve. Yet I have forgiven myself because God has forgiven me and showed me how to move forward with healthy perspectives about my past and the choices I made. I remember coming home from prison and my mom dying shortly thereafter. It was devastating. I actually watched my mom die moment after moment, day after day. It took a lot out of me. I was still a young girl and I had always depended on my mom as a backbone. To see her in this state was devastating to me. It also made me realize that I needed to grow up quick and in a hurry. My siblings and me had always depended on my mom and counted on her being there.

Nevertheless she was gone. I still hadn't learned my lesson about living life on the streets. I continued to sell drugs, smoking weed, gang bangin, and doing my own thing. I had been to jail enough now were being in a relationship with a woman seemed normal to me and I began to prefer that over being in a relationship with a man. This is where the lesbian lifestyle was introduced to me.

In the beginning, I looked at these women involved with other women like they were out of their minds. I would say things like "She thinks she's a man" while pointing my finger. Now, here I am right in the midst of it all and I'm in the same category as they are. A bonified lesbian. Most of the women I was surrounded by would always say things to convince me to get involved like hey girl you're pretty do you want to be my girlfriend or hey you're just my type pretty and sexy. You know how it starts, you do something once and then you don't stop, before you know it you're in too deep and now you're a dedicated member

It was something I took very serious and I became dedicated to the lifestyle. I would be in a relationship and if I really liked that person I would tattoo their name on my body as a symbol of our love. This began to be a repeated cycle for me. I found myself in several relationships and as a result I tattooed three names on my body as a representation of our relationship. Then, I began to live my life on the streets as a lesbian, yeah I had a point to prove and I couldn't' go back to the real Holli.

At that time I didn't care what anybody had to say or who didn't approve of it. I was a full fledged lesbian; club hopping, pants sagging, thuggin', actively involved in the activities the lesbian lifestyle offered.

I spent many weekends' club hopping and partying going to all the hang out spots for lesbians. They would look up to you, and try to immolate your style. I had a point to prove and now I had developed this resentment for all men. Although it really was a façade to hide all the hurt I had experienced, I needed to be this new person to escape the past. Now that I can look back on my choices clearly, I realize that the hurt and pain was still there while living that lifestyle and it only got worse.

I became this dominant fearless bulldagger and in my head I was now a man. I began to dress like a man, baggy jeans, boxer shorts; I cut off all my hair, died it blonde and sported a bald fade. My friends who were in the same category I was in as far as lesbians are concerned, we would call each other boy. Like when we greeted one another we would say "what's up boy". There are a couple of categories you fall in with this lifestyle. Either you are a feminine girl or you are very aggressive like a man. I was the very aggressive type. I had been a "tomboy" all my life and it seemed fitting to act as a man.

I was deep into the lifestyle and there was no changing my mind. I was sexually involved with women and in the lesbian lifestyle most women still want to be penetrated, so I would use toys to satisfy their desires. I was the type that denied the penetration, in my mind it was as if I allowed a man on top of me and that was a no-no! Plus in this lifestyle if you allowed that you were considered soft or a bitch! In my mind it was all about doing everything that was considered to be protocol for the lesbian lifestyle. That's how you got props from your peers. They would look up to you, and try to immolate your style. After all, I had an image to keep up; there was this sense of having something to belong to like a family. People knew me. They respected me. The men who hit on me I made it clear to them that they had nothing coming. "I wanted what they wanted".

This is what I would say to them. I turned into this person that I never knew could exist. People showed me love. Basically, we were all the same at some point; in need of love and a place we could call home to escape our true feelings. A way to be someone else and not ourselves so we could hide the hurt, pain or confusion we had experienced at some point that lead to our current choices. Now that I understand why I behaved like that, when I see someone in the lesbian or gay lifestyle, I hurt for them, I hear their silent cry. I pray for them and treat them with love and respect. I want so badly to see them delivered and set free.

During the course of time while making these changes living as a lesbian my children was there to witness this person I had become. They didn't understand it. It was forced upon them. This new mother, I didn't realize that I had abandoned their needs and put my selfish desires before theirs.

Boy when I realized what I had done, I cried so hard. I have always loved my boys; I just didn't know how to express that love in a healthy way because of the hurt and pain I suffered and a lack of knowledge.

I thought that as long as I kept them with the latest gear, Michael Jordan gym shoes and gave them what they wanted I was showing them love.

I would cook and clean on a regular basis because that's the way I was raised, but making sure they got all the hugs and kisses and spending enough quality time with them I didn't do. Yes I spent lots of time with them but it's a whole lot different when you give a child your undivided attention. That I wasn't doing. I was too busy satisfying my own personal desires. I was in one relationship after another, inviting different women to move in with me and the boys, not thinking about the lifestyle I was living before them. I remember my second son Jeremy said to me one day "when I grow up I ain't gone be gay".

Every time they looked up, they had a new brother or sister due to my relationships. One after another, it started to be a pattern, I began to experience the same hurt, pain and drama that I had went through with a man. One day I realized that my desire for men was not dead I had just buried it deep down inside of me because to me it was tied to hurt, pain and disappointment. I never wanted to feel those emotions again.

There was this guy who was very special to me. We grew up together and hung out a lot with each other. His mom was my big brother's girlfriend when we were kids. When we got older we started to admire one another and he showed me so much love and attention, we would sell drugs together and "hook up". Suddenly he moved out of town.

I know I wasn't the reason he moved out of town, he wanted a better life for himself so he decided that he would move to where he had family in another state and he could get away from the negative environment.

Whenever he came to town he would look for me, I had a special lust for him. I would do things with him that I wouldn't dare do with another guy. We shared something so special, He wanted more but I refused to put myself in a vulnerable position again.

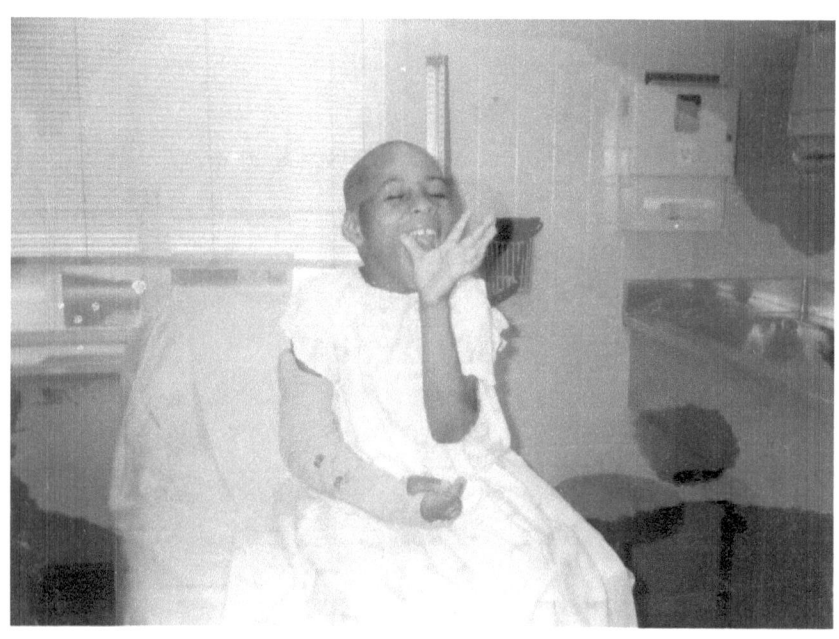

Jeremy Hunt

I had given us some thought as far as establishing a real relationship, but I had gotten so comfortable with living as a lesbian and I didn't know how to give that lifestyle up. I was convinced that this was now who I was suppose to be. I figured I could be in control of the relationships I indulged in and therefore control how the relationships would unravel. This way I would never have to face the drama from the past.

That was just all bull. I continued to find myself in relationships full of drama and disappointments. The same ole cycle of hurt, headaches and drama was still present. In this particular moment in my life things were going well (so I thought). I had just gotten a new place and making good money and decided shortly after that to move together with my new female companion. We moved together and very shortly after that my second son died. This was a very tough moment for me. I remember every second of that day as if it were yesterday. To make matters worse, it was on April fool's day, 1998.

Boy this was a heavy blow to me, his dad, and my family. To add to the hurt, the doctors couldn't give me a definite answer as to how he died. They just said that someone coughed or sneezed in his face. Wow what a blow. I'll never forget hearing my own son tell me "mama I'm gonna die"! There was nothing I could do to help him. I lost it after hearing those words. I was escorted from the room and about 30 minutes later, they tell me my son is dead. I didn't know what to do or who to call on. I would continuously listen to this gospel song I had heard while riding in the car with my brother. This song was an encouragement for me.

Even though I didn't really understand what the words meant, it was definitely a source of strength. He was the kinda kid everybody liked. He was such a sweetheart. He would open and hold doors for me; he would fix me sandwiches and kool-aid. He was also the type that didn't take no mess. My boys had a basketball game and we used to shoot hoops inside the house when it was cold outside and he could shoot like 20 straight without missing. He was a great student in school and math was his favorite subject. He was a charmer.

Well I didn't know exactly how, but I began to move on with life as I knew it. I remember feeling like I wanted something different for my life. I just didn't know how to go about making that happen. As a result, I got right back to selling drugs and doing my own thing. Soon afterwards, I got into some trouble and got arrested for drug possession. This was it for me!

At the same time I had a job doing home care service and yet I really wanted a change. I was in a relationship that was basically draining all of my energy. This woman was very insecure and she wanted to keep tabs on my every move. I got drama from her 24/7. She would pull out some of her weave and call the police and say I hit her. She was full of drama. She would change the locks when I would go out and come back late. She liked to argue and fight in public and she had to make known to everybody who she was to me. I remember my older brother saying to me one day that she had a one track mind and Holli Hunt was written all over it. It was a very stressful time in my life. I started to contemplate on my life and the choices I had been making. Realizing the need for a change, I stopped smoking marijuana and drinking and selling drugs. That was very easy for me to do. However, I still had to face the drug charges and find a way to walk away from all the negativity in my life.

CHAPTER 2

The Conqueror

As time progressed, I began living my life without selling drugs or smoking marijuana, yet I was still active in the club life and being a lesbian. I remember one morning going to court for the drug possession charges and being apprehended. Boy did things change in such a way.

Now here I am incarcerated, my 2 boys are left behind and I could be facing a lot of time. I'm in jail now for a while and I found out that my female companion had left my boys in the house by them selves and skipped out on us. She had just kicked me to the curb while letting some other women drive her around in my car. That made me do a lot more thinking. Anyway I remember getting down on my knees one day and asking God to help me and to change me because I never wanted to be away from my boys ever again and if He would I would walk away from everything and do right by Him.

During that same time I had started relationships with the women who were incarcerated with me. Shortly after that I remember having enough of it all. I was changing, I didn't desire to do the things I used to do, and I didn't desire to be in relationships with women anymore. It was happening right before my eyes. I didn't want to sit around playing cards, talking smack, and watching videos on the TV. This time, I really had enough of it all. I met a woman who used to pray with me and talk to me all the time about making changes with my life. This was a real friendship, something I wasn't used to at all. I never really had a lot of female friends because I was a tomboy all my life and I was always hangin with the fellows. My mom used to tell me when I was coming up as a kid that when I hung with a crowd of boys, the only way she knew who I was by looking down at my feet because I'm pigeon-toed and bow-legged. I have a few friends that are still near and dear to my heart, but this relationship was different. It was like a soul sista kinda relationship, a spiritual connection. God was doing for me what I couldn't do for myself. He put someone in my life to be that help, that support because He had plans for my life. I remember being rude and disruptive when the people from different churches in the city would visit the jail to pray with the inmates and have church services.

Now I had started to listen to the things they would say and they would also pray with me. Anyway, as time progressed, I continued to read my Bible but more on a consistent basis. I started to believe what it said about me and who I really was as a child of God.

In Romans 8, verses 14-16:

For all who are led by the Spirit of God are sons of God.

For [the Spirit which] you have now received [is] not s spirit of slavery to put you once more in bondage to fear, but you have received the Spirit of adoption [the Spirit producing sonship] in [the bliss of] shich we cry Abba (Father)! Father!

The Spirit Himself [thus] testifies together with our own spirit, [assuring us] that we are children of God.

The word adoption means sonship: adopted sons share the same rights and priviledges as one born in the family.

Then I read in Galatians 3, verse26:

For in Christ Jesus you are all sons of God through faith.

I also read in Jeremiah 29:11

For I know the thoughts and plans that I have for you, says the Lord, thoughts and plans for welfare and peace and not for evil, to give you hope in your final outcome.

I also read in 1 Peter 2:9-11

But you are a chosen race, a royal priesthood, a dedicated nation, [God's] own purchased, special people, that you may set forth the wonderful deeds and display the virtues and perfections of Him Who called you out f darkness into His marvelous light.

Once you were not a people [at all], but now you are God's people; once you were unpitied, but now you are pitied and have received mercy.

Beloved, I implore you as aliens and strangers and exiles [in this world] to abstain from the sensual urges (the evil desires, the passions of the flesh, your lower nature) that wage war against the soul.

Before I surrendered and gave my life unto God I was a mess and didn't have direction about life or understand who I should be as a child of God. Now that I had started to understand what God was saying about my life, I believed Him and wanted to know what is was like to be royalty. I started to understand that I had a responsibility after I had read His Word and was enlightened with truth to then be obedient. Its one thing not to understand but when you understand you can take action. It's like that old saying 'when you know better you do better'. I had to give up my fleshly desires and passions and seek to have my soul cleansed of those evils. I wanted to be royalty and behave like a queen. I began to feel like it, and the desire to be a woman again was slowly emerging.

I started wearing pants that fit, make-up, growing my hair back, and I gave up my gangster limp for a sexy strut. I was beginning to come into my own as Holli, the Holli I was born to be. The Holli that God had preordained me to be before the foundations of this world.

Yes it was still tough for me because I had haters on every side watching my every move trying to make me look bad and keep me from moving forward. Plus this was something I had never attempted to do. People would say things like 'she got that jail house religion'. Little did they know I was not playing anymore games with my life?

Not only that, I had made a promise to God and I knew that this was serious business for me. I had to be a woman of my word and that's just what I planned on doing.

This not being a lesbian anymore was tougher than I thought. The minute I decided to stop living this way women would write me letters trying to convince me to be in a relationship with them, all my ex-girlfriends started visiting me, and this girl who I was previously dealing with, I told her that I didn't want a relationship anymore and we had to separate.

So we separated for about 3 or 4 days. I didn't expect her to come back on me with the let's just be friends scheme. Little did I know that this was a set up by the enemy to get me back in his grips? I agreed with just being friends and before I knew it, I was right back in the relationship. But I was still praying to God every night and asking Him for strength and to help me.

My friend, (my soul sista) reminded me that I couldn't be friends with the enemy and that he will always have some control like that. So I ended all ties with my companion and boy did this create some tension. She got so angry and didn't want to accept what I wanted. Nevertheless I was so serious about what I wanted and I truly wanted out. You see I had realized that I needed to make the first move and be obedient to God's Word. From the book of James 4:7 I had to resist the enemy and then he would flee.

Once I resisted the enemy with the strength that was already inside of me then God would grant more strength to continue to defeat this giant. I didn't know that I had the strength to do such a thing. I had to dig deep down inside of me and use the God-given strength I already had. You see I had to give myself unto God and then expect His promise to be fulfilled that the devil would flee. All God's promises are designed for those who believe in God's power. Plus there was a mental strength that I had to use to embrace the truth about whom God said I was and who I could become through Him.

In the book of Romans, the 8th chapter and the 37th verse it says that *Yet amid all these things we are more than conquerors and gain a surpassing victory through*

Him Who loved us. I also read in the book of Deuteronomy, 32:10 that I was *the apple of God's eye.* Someone that is very special to God, someone he would watch over, instruct and be my keeper. This scripture was the assurance that God truly loved me.

It was crucial that I develop a different mindset about the way I perceived things; I needed to renew my mind, renew my thinking. The only way to renew your mind is with the Word of God. Once you have a new way of thinking, your actions will change as well. Most importantly, I needed to get to the root of the problem that had lead to my actions. I needed to find out why was I behaving as such and what caused me to behave like that.

After doing research I learned that I was behaving the way I was because of spirits that had invaded me internally and perverted my thinking and as these spirits continued to live within me they grew stronger and stronger and I couldn't control them. I started to believe the evil things he said I was, rather I heard it from my peers, on the television or read it in some magazine. If ever there's a time of negative thinking, we allow the enemy to pervade our thinking and seduce us with evil spirits to take control over our choices and ultimately our lives and his goal is to kill, steal and destroy.

One of the spirits is the spirit of lust. Lust—#1. Sexual craving. #2. Any overwhelming craving.—v. To have an inordinate desire.

You see I had developed an inordinate desire that wasn't natural. It was out of the proper order of how God created us to carry ourselves and to indulge in relationships. God's order is man with woman and not anything contrary. This spirit was out to destroy me. The more I participated in the activities, the stronger the spirit got, until I was under it's power and couldn't control my actions. Not only did lust consume me but it altered my beliefs about myself. I didn't have the esteem about myself I should've. My self-esteem was already at an ultimate low before I ever got involved in the lifestyle. I never knew that it was okay to be me and that I was valuable and that I was special. I was no longer comfortable being Holli so I started to be someone else. I was never sure about who I was. But I learned the truth and I was not allowing nothing and nobody to deter my thinking and my beliefs.

You see what ever you believe you act from that belief so I started thinking positive about myself and the woman I should and could be.

What helped me to understand that I needed to think positive was the scripture I found in the book of Phillippians in the 4th chapter and the 8th verse.

For the rest, brethren, whatever is true, whatever is worthy of reverence and is honorable and seemly, whatever is just, whatever is pure, whatever is lovely and lovable, whatever is kind and winsome and gracious, if there is any virtue and excellence, if there is anything worthy of praise, think on and weigh and take account for these things [fix you minds on them].

You see I had to think positive no matter what. Another major responsibility was for me to distance myself from anybody that was active in that lifestyle because that was just temptation and I wasn't strong enough to be in their presence and not be a part of the same activities. It's like saying you want to get off drugs but you find yourself in a dope house everyday where drug users are. That's not a form of strength. You must sever all ties with anyone in that lifestyle. Yes that's one of the toughest parts but when you want greater for your life sometimes you must get rid of people, places and things in order to move forward effectively.

This evil wants to consume and kill you so you must strategize against it and follow through. Scriptures teach us that we only receive what we believe. We must believe in our future and the person we're supposed to be. I started to believe that I was born to be a woman and not a man and that I were supposed to have relationships with men and not women.

I believed in the writings of the apostle Paul that I am more than a conqueror through Him who loves me. This is what kept me focused and empowered me to persevere no matter what. We must have a form of strength to conquer this evil.

While you distance yourself for a good period of time you must arm yourself with prayer, keep the company of strong positive people and trust in God to strengthen you to be victorious. Then you will see change on a consistent basis.

Later on, after my ex saw me in action she was able to accept the new me. Months later we were on speaking terms again which was good but I knew I wasn't ready for us to be friends again. After some time you may be able to have friends in that lifestyle but then make sure you're strong enough and that only you do the persuading and no one persuades or dictate your actions. I remember being in church one day and someone passed me a note. It was from some girl wanting me to start a relationship with her. I took the note after reading it; I folded it up and wrote on the top part where she could see it *THE BLOOD OF JESUS* then I sent it back to her. That's when I knew that God was really real, His Word became alive to me and His Word had imparted the strength I needed to keep saying no. I was truly on my way towards a new life. Some people may accept it and some may not but we must not allow anyone to stop us. Then I remember getting a visit from a dear friend. She was one of my closest friends that I had from the lesbian lifestyle. She was freaking out when she saw the changes I was making and when I told her I never would be a lesbian again she said 'well I am' that never stopped me from moving forward and going after what I really wanted for my life. I wasn't mad or angry with her; I just knew that I had to make this choice for myself. I knew that no one could make this choice for me; it was solely up to me. There will be some people who love you no matter what.

They will be the ones encouraging you to keep going, Anyway, a little while later, I went to court and was sentenced to 10 years. This was devastating! I was hoping to come home after being in the county jail for about 14 months away from my boys and family. This was a hard pill to swallow. Nevertheless, it was a pill that I had to swallow.

All I kept thinking about was how am I gonna be without my boys all that time? Who was gonna take care of them and how hurt they were gonna be when they found out that they had to be without their momma for so many more years. I kept things to myself for as long as I could because I really didn't want my boys to be hurt more than they already were. I just couldn't build up the courage to tell them the news. As time went on my cousin, the one who was keeping and taking care of them began to demand what was going on with me. So I told her the news and of course she and the family and my kids were devastated. At this point I knew I had to do all that I could to be a woman of my word. To keep my promise I made to God. I met a very special lady and she began to be a mentor to me. She helped me in so many ways. We would sit and read and study the Bible together, self-educating ourselves in every way possible. Doing all we could do to prepare ourselves to re-enter society and be the mothers that we should have been all along.

Again, God was continuously looking out for me. He put someone in my path to help me because again He had plans for my life. I had to rid the spirit of religion and learn to be a "Kingdom Representative". She was mainly a spiritual mother to me. She demonstrated that strength that I needed to see and obtain in order to move in the path that God had designed for me. She taught me a lot about life and being a woman. I had to learn the basics; how to posture myself while sitting and standing, eating like a lady, conducting a conversation like a lady, there was so much that I had allowed to slip away from me. There's was so much I had buried.

When I was a lesbian, I just wanted to dress and look good not taking pride in the woman I was born to be, but trying to immolate the actions of a man. I wore men cologne and did basically most of the things a man would do. Anyway, we would put together special projects to edify and encourage the women we were incarcerated with. There was no stopping us. We were on a mission.

I began to be conscious about my appearance as far as my physical health was concerned, and my skin and hair. I began to take pride in the woman I was and didn't care what others had to say. I had a tough time back in the county lock-up when people would say things it would bother me, but I got stronger and stronger and there was no stopping this new Holli. I had realized that life was not over for me and that this was my opportunity to start all over and pursue my dreams and aspirations.

I began to evolve as a woman and even though I was surrounded by at least 1200 to 1500 women, the desire to be in a relationship with one was dead. I would have inmate friends that would ask me to meet with them because they needed to talk. They wanted to be delivered but don't know what to do or how to even begin to get away from this way of life. I would just encourage them and at that time, I really didn't say much more. I was determined to let my actions speak for me. I never looked at another woman inappropriate. That lesbian life I had lived and was accustomed to for approximately 10 years was history. Thank You Jesus!

I was now on my way toward a big and bright future and looking forward to reuniting with my boys and being the mother they deserved and needed so desperately. I began to make plans for our future and doing all I could to follow through. Trusting in God to care for them in my absence and be their mother and father.

My prayer life got stronger and I started to pray for God to go before me and set my path and make a way for all our needs and want to be met upon my release from prison. God did just that! A couple days after I got released, I got a job, and two months later, I had my own apartment and my own car. Things were beginning to look up for us. My goal was to get that bond back with my boys and do all I could to earn their trust. We would go to the basketball court and shoot, go out to eat, play video games together, all kind of things to learn them over again, the young men they have become. I wouldn't date for a year, almost two. I refused to give my undivided attention to anyone but them. I was on a mission!

There's no such thing as parenting behind bars, children need their parents in person to be their guides and role models, give them lots of hugs and kisses, tell them you love them everyday, and to tuck them in at night. You can write all the letters you want and demand that they are on their best behavior but they are hurt and they're doing time too.

That absence creates a big hole in their hearts and some kids need counseling and some go astray. They are subjected to so much and because they lack that needed attention, they look for it from others. Not to say that their caregivers are not doing a good job it's just a big risk to be doing your own thing and living a selfish lifestyle not considering the consequences and all who will suffer from those consequences.

Before you know it, they're following in your footsteps and there isn't much you can say to change their minds about the lifestyle they have chosen. I've learned that the enemy will always try to tempt our children with the same evil he has tempted the parents with. If he's gotten away with it before, he wants to keep going through the family and attacking our seed, this is one of the ways he tries to keep the parents bound and burdened and ultimately seeking to destroy us all. If he doesn't have his grips on the parent any longer, he will strongly attempt to get his grips on our children. This was true for me; I started getting phone calls in prison concerning my oldest son Kerron, he had started getting involved in the same things I had gotten involved in as a teenager.

He dropped out of school and began to do his own thing, started gang bangin' stealing to smoke marijuana with his so called friends. This activity and peer pressure soon forced him to step his game up. He got off the chain for the devil.

No one wanted to see him coming, none of my family that is. He would visit them and steal from them and he had started to carry guns and got deeper involved in the gang lifestyle. Once I arrived, he had already made up his mind as to the lifestyle he was gonna lead. I tried so hard to be that role model and express the love that he needed but there was this resentment he had bottled inside of him for me and his dad. He felt like he was on his own and he had to be that man that society had labeled him to be.

I had to deal with the fighting and gangbangin in school, I transferred him at least 3 times to different schools hoping to encourage him to go back to the way he was living before he was ever intrigued by the lifestyle he was now living. He used to be an A. student. Very active in sports and he could play basketball very good. He was very gifted with his hands. He knew wires and

Kerron Hunt

could fix anything. He could clean better than any woman I knew. But he had totally changed. Unfortunately, it was too late. He had a point to prove and a name to live up to. Even though he chose this lifestyle, there was still this special love he showed toward me and I could see the hurt and disappointment in his eyes.

He was disappointed in me for leaving him. Basically it was like him having to grow up and be the man of the house now that I was gone. This was too much pressure for any kid. Then, the woman I showed back up as he wasn't used to so he really didn't know how to handle that or how to embrace that. In his eyes I had changed and he thought that I would show back up and be his partner in crime. Nevertheless, as time progressed things got worse, I started hearing things about his behavior and people would be looking for him to hurt him. It was a time of chaos. Well I had been released for a while now, it was 2007 and at this point Kerron and my relationship was good but he didn't come around much because he knew that I wouldn't turn my head to the lifestyle he was living and he didn't want to hear me fuss at him about doing something with his life. I continued to pray everyday on my family's behalf and yet the unexpected happened!

Once again I must bury a son, this time my oldest son, Kerron Rasheem Hunt. He was shot and killed in the same month my second son Jeremy Terrell Hunt got sick and died in, April.

When I got the news I just threw my hands up and said "naked I came into this world and naked shall I leave, to God be the glory"! Boy this hurt and pain I never thought I would have to face again was here and stronger than ever! It was as if my heart got ran over by an 18 wheeler! There was this feeling in my gut that I just couldn't shake. All the while, I knew I had to be strong for my only living son Donnell.

This was such a trying time for both of us but I'm grateful to be able to say that if God hadn't been with me, I would definitely be in an institution bangin my head against the wall. God saturated me with His Power and comfort in such a way. I can't explain how I was able to deal with burying two sons. I know in my heart it was God's peace and joy that lived deep inside of me. During that time I felt His presence so strong as if I literally was bathing in it. I remember how tough it was for Donnell, he couldn't sleep at night so he would sleep with me. This went on for at least a month. Then one day God made me realize that I couldn't allow the spirit of fear to live in my house. So I sat Donnell down and told him that I know how bad he's hurting but we were gonna be okay. I told him that God is with us and that he didn't have to be afraid and nothing was gonna happen to him or me. So I said tonight you're gonna sleep in your own bed and you're gonna be okay. If you can't sleep keep praying because the spirit of fear can no longer live here! Now, things are getting better for Donnell and me as a family, God continues to keep His hand on our lives and He takes very good care of us.

Donnell is now a junior in high school, college bound, a very bright and respectful young man. He's gifted in music and he's the linebacker on the school football team. He has big goals and dreams set for his life and I'm gonna do all within my power to help them manifest.

As for me, I'm a living witness that God answers prayers and that making the choice to participate in the homosexual lifestyle and in any lifestyle that's not right before the eyes of God can be conquered and you can experience total liberation if you call on The Almighty God and trust Him for His delivering power. God is real and I'm a living witness as to what He can do. I have learned some very valuable lessons from my experiences and choices and one of the main lessons is that I am somebody and I can be me and nobody else can be me but me and Life's great being me. I don't have to be somebody else today I'm very comfortable and very sure about who I am and who's I am. Thank You JESUS! I'm now waiting for Mr. Right to come along and still making good on my word and promise to God: living to advance the Kingdom of God in every way possible. Being a servant, doing all I can in my power to live an unselfish lifestyle of excellence and putting others before me and keeping in check any desire that's not like God by His Grace and Mercies. I hope to open up a shelter for battered women and children someday in the near future. I'm working on my third book, writing songs and working hard to produce and release my first gospel CD.

All scripture were taken from the Holy Bible, the King James Version, 1963, The Amplified Version, 1958 and all definitions from the Strong's Concordance, 1886.

For those of you who read this book allow me to say thank you for your time and support. I pray that you were touched, empowered and enlightened. I love you and I pray that you would come to know the depth, height and width of God's love.

This book is dedicated to the memory of my mom, Joan Patricia McKee, my two sons Kerron Rasheem Hunt and Jeremy Terrell Hunt, my brother Kevin McKee and nephew Corey Hunt. They will never be forgotten because of the life I live and their spirits that live on through me.

Special Thanks: to Rev. Calvin Brown, Erna and Eric Hunt, Geraldine Smith, Vicki and Roy Elzy and my son Donnell for your continuous unconditional love and support. You are greatly appreciated.

Kingdom Steward,
Holli J. Hunt

www.ingramcontent.com/pod-product-compliance
Lightning Source LLC
Chambersburg PA
CBHW061220280526
45784CB00006B/2570